REMARKABLE PEOPLE

David Beckham

by Galadriel Watson

Published by Weigl Publishers Inc.
350 5th Avenue, Suite 3304, PMB 6G
New York, NY 10118-0069

Website: www.weigl.com

Library of Congress Cataloging-in-Publication Data

Watson, Galadriel Findlay.
David Beckham / Galadriel Watson.
p. cm. -- (Remarkable people)
Includes index.
ISBN 978-1-59036-641-7 (hard cover : alk. paper) -- ISBN 978-1-59036-642-4 (soft cover : alk. paper)
1. Beckham, David, 1975---Juvenile literature. 2. Soccer players--England--Biography--Juvenile literature. 3. Celebrities--England--Biography--Juvenile literature. I. Title.
GV942.7.B432W38 2008
796.334092--dc22
[B]

2006039439

Printed in the United States of America
1 2 3 4 5 6 7 8 9 0 11 10 09 08 07

Editor: Leia Tait
Design: Terry Paulhus

Cover: David Beckham is an example for young athletes around the world.

Photograph Credits
© John Jones JDJ Communications: pages 6, 8, 9.

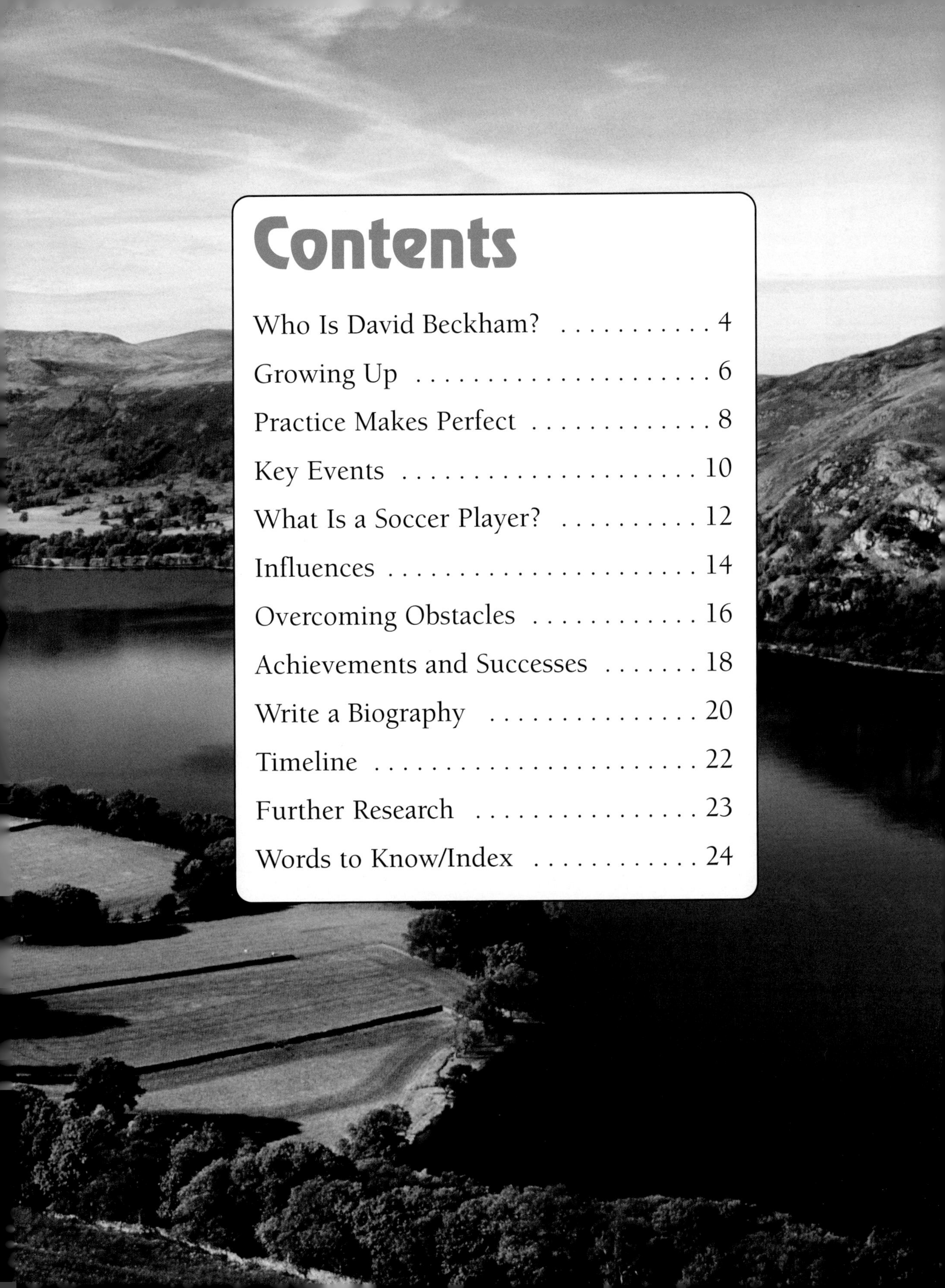

Contents

Who Is David Beckham?

David Beckham plays soccer. He is one of the world's most successful **professional** athletes. He began playing soccer at the professional level in 1991. David became well-known in 1996 when he kicked a goal from the middle of the soccer field. For most of his career, David played with the Manchester United team. This team is based in the city of Manchester, England. From 2000 to 2006, David was also the captain of England's national soccer team. He now plays for the Los Angeles Galaxy in California. David is well-known around the world for his impressive soccer skills.

"There was only one thing I ever wanted to do with my life."

Growing Up

David Robert Joseph Beckham was born on May 2, 1975, in Leytonstone, England. England is part of Great Britain. As soon as he could walk, David's father, Ted, gave him a soccer ball to kick around. When David was three, he received a Manchester United uniform for Christmas. David often wore his Manchester uniform while practicing soccer.

David has two sisters, Lynne and Joanne. When David would play soccer in the back garden, Joanne would play **goalie**. David's parents, Sandra and Ted, were both great soccer fans. Ted played for the local soccer club. David loved to watch his father play.

As a child, David dreamed of becoming a professional soccer player.

Get to Know Great Britain

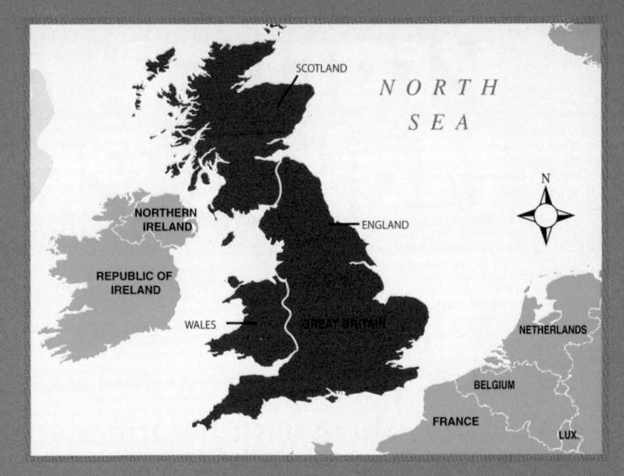

ENGLAND

SCOTLAND

WALES

The island of Great Britain includes England, Scotland, and Wales.

Great Britain and Northern Ireland together make up the United Kingdom.

Great Britain is the eighth-largest island in the world.

London is the capital of Great Britain.

The lion is an important symbol in Great Britain. British rulers kept these great cats in their castles 800 years ago.

David lived in Great Britain until he was 28 years of age. Then he moved to Spain. Imagine moving to a different country. Make a chart comparing your home to another country. Compare things like language, weather, food, clothing, jobs, and nature. What new things would you need to learn about your new home?

Practice Makes Perfect

David put much effort into practicing his soccer skills. He often practiced with his father at a park near his house. David also played soccer there with his friends. Some of the kids David played with were much older than him. They wanted to play with David because he was so good at soccer.

David often played soccer with his father's team at the local soccer club. He trained with the adults and played **matches** with them for fun. At the club, David practiced kicking the soccer ball towards the goal. Each time he was able to hit the **crossbar**, David's dad gave him a pat on the back and some extra spending money.

Young David exercised to become stronger and improve his soccer skills.

When David was 7 years old, he joined the Ridgeway Rovers. This was a new youth soccer team in his neighborhood. By the following year, David had scored more than 100 goals with the Rovers.

David played soccer with the Rovers for six years. During that time, he also played for his district and **county** teams. He traveled to many new places. David learned a great deal about soccer and continued to improve at the sport. **Scouts** from professional teams started watching him. They were impressed by his skills and knowledge of the sport. David worked very hard, hoping his favorite team—Manchester United—would hear about him.

QUICK FACTS

- Manchester United are known as the Red Devils. They wear a devil on their team logo.
- As a child, David enjoyed music, drawing, painting, and swimming.
- When David was 11, he competed against 100 other young soccer players from the United Kingdom to win the Bobby Charlton Soccer Schools National Skills Competition.

David met one of his heroes, Bobby Charlton, after winning the National Skills Competition. Bobby was once a star player for Manchester United.

Key Events

When David was 14, his dream came true. Manchester United asked him to start training with them. David was thrilled. In 1991, when he was 16, David officially joined Manchester United's junior team. On April 2, 1995, he played his first **Premier League** game. In 1996, David scored a spectacular goal from the middle of the field in a match against Wimbledon. Overnight, he became a soccer star. That one kick changed his life.

David played for Manchester United for 10 years. During that time, he also played for England's national soccer team. He served as England's team captain from 2000 to 2006. In 2003, David left Manchester United to play for Spain's Real Madrid team. He stayed in Spain until 2007. That year, David joined the Los Angeles Galaxy. This is a Major League Soccer team in Los Angeles, California. As the best-known soccer star in the world, David brings a great deal of attention to the sport in the United States.

On Manchester United and England's national team, David wore number 7. While playing for Real Madrid, he wore number 23.

Thoughts from David

David has loved soccer ever since he was a child. Here are some things he has said about the sport and his life.

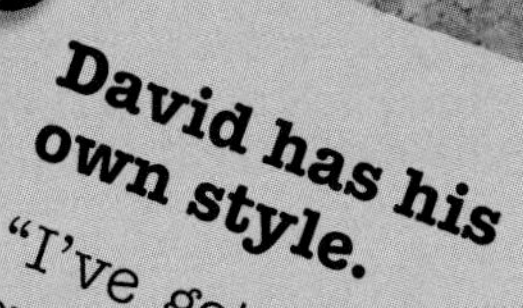

David has his own style.

"I've got my own tastes and if I can indulge them I will."

David joins the Los Angeles Galaxy.

"I look forward to the new challenge of growing the world's most popular game in a country that is as passionate about its sports as my own."

David is thankful for his parents' support when he was young.

"If there was a way for me to get to a game, they did everything they could to make it happen."

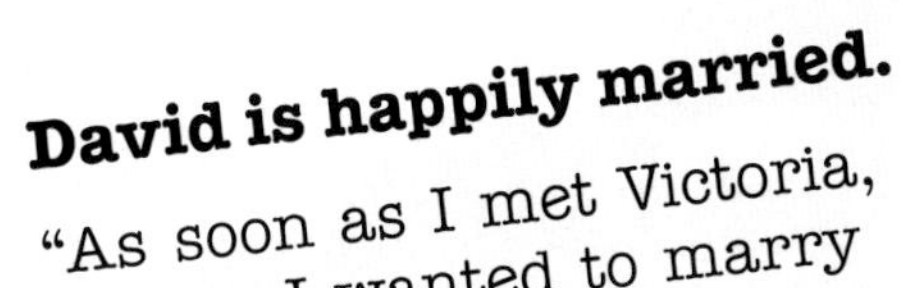

David is happily married.

"As soon as I met Victoria, I knew I wanted to marry her, to have children, to be together always."

Ten-year-old David is unable to play soccer because of an injury.

"That was the longest five weeks of my life."

David enjoys being a father.

"I walk into the house and, as soon as I'm with the boys, nothing else matters but them."

What Is a Soccer Player?

Soccer is a team sport. In other parts of the world, including Great Britain, it is often called football. Soccer is a popular sport to play because it has simple rules. It does not require much equipment. Soccer is played with a round ball on a rectangular field. There is a goal at each end of the field. Each match has two teams. There are 11 players on each team. During the game, players have to kick the ball into the other team's goal. The team with the most goals wins.

Each player on a soccer team has a specific role. Some move the ball around the field. Others are good at scoring goals. Some try to stop members of the other team from scoring. All professional soccer players train to be the best at what they do. The most important **tournament** they play is the World Cup. It takes place every four years.

More than 240 million people in 200 countries play soccer.

Soccer Players 101

Pelé (1940–)

Team: Brazilian National Team
Achievements: Edson Arantes do Nascimento is better known by his nickname, Pelé. He was the first soccer player to become a superstar. He has been called "The King of Soccer." Pelé was born in Brazil and grew up very poor. He began playing on a local soccer team when he was 15. Soon, Pelé began playing professional soccer. In 1958, at the age of 17, Pelé played in his first World Cup tournament. He scored six goals and became well known. Pelé scored more than 1,000 goals. In 1999, he was named the International Olympic Committee Athlete of the Century.

Hristo Stoitchkov (1966–)

Team: Bulgarian National Team
Achievements: Stoitchkov was born in Bulgaria. He has played for many teams, including Barcelona in Spain and Kashiwa Reysol in Japan. Stoitchkov became well known after his team won the Spanish Primera Division four times in a row. He helped his team win the Champions League in 1992. Stoitchkov was the top scorer in the 1994 World Cup. He is sometimes known as "Raging Bull" or "the Mad Bulgarian." Stoitchkov was Bulgarian Player of the Year from 1989 to 1992, and in 1994.

Zinedine Zidane (1972–)

Team: French National Team
Achievements: Zidane was born in France. His family moved there from Algeria. Zidane played his first professional game at the age of 17. He has won many trophies. These include the UEFA Cup, the European Supercup, and the Intercontinental Cup. Zidane joined the Real Madrid team in 2001. Real Madrid paid $66 million for Zidane to join their team. Zidane was awarded the **FIFA** World Player of the Year Award in 1998, 2000, and 2003.

Mia Hamm (1972–)

Team: U.S. National Team
Achievements: Many people think Hamm is the world's best female soccer player. She was born in North Carolina. When she was 15, Hamm became the youngest player to play with the United States National Women's Team. In 1996, she helped the United States' team win gold at the Olympic Games. Hamm has scored more goals in international competition than any other soccer player in history. She won ESPN's Female Athlete of the Year in 1998 and 1999. In 2001 and 2002, Hamm received the FIFA Women's World Player of the Year Award.

The Soccer Ball

The outside of a soccer ball is made with **synthetic** leather. It usually has 32 panels. The inside of the ball, which holds the air, is called the bladder. There are many types of soccer balls. Some are used by professional players. Others are made for practice or for playing indoors. Soccer balls come in different sizes. Smaller balls are for young children.

Influences

David has had two main influences in his life. These are his family and his coaches. When David was about eight, his father stopped playing soccer. Instead, he wanted to spend his time coaching David. David says Ted taught him many of the skills that helped him become an excellent soccer player. Ted taught David courage, commitment, energy, and **vision**. He showed David that it is important to be able to inspire other players.

While David played for the Ridgeway Rovers, his mother spent many hours driving the team around. David's parents helped out the team by washing uniforms and fundraising. They paid for David to attend soccer schools. They also took him to watch many soccer matches.

Coaches make decisions during games and help players learn skills. Sir Alex Ferguson was David's first professional coach. He has been the coach of Manchester United since 1986.

David has praised his coaches. He said that the Ridgeway Rovers' coach was tough but talented. Players had to train twice a week. If they missed a training session, they were not allowed to play on the weekend. This taught David to be present and on time. He learned that soccer was about **teamwork**, not about showing off his skills.

THE BECKHAM FAMILY

David married Victoria Adams in 1999. Victoria is known as Posh Spice. She sang with a pop music group called the Spice Girls. David and Victoria are well known around the world. Their nicknames are "Posh" and "Becks." David and Victoria have three sons. Brooklyn was born in 1999. Romeo was born in 2002. Their youngest, Cruz, was born in 2005. David is often busy traveling and playing soccer, but he spends as much time as he can with his family. He has even **tattooed** their names on his body.

David and Victoria work hard to balance their careers and their family.

Overcoming Obstacles

Being a top athlete has not been easy for David. He has faced many challenges. As a child and teenager, David was very small. No matter how much he ate, he could not gain weight. Some coaches thought David was not strong enough to play soccer. However, he often played with bigger, older kids. David also played with his Dad's soccer teammates. He learned to avoid being injured by stronger players.

David's personal life has been difficult sometimes. Since he is a celebrity, David and his family receive a great deal of attention. Photographers and **journalists** often follow David and his family when they leave their home. Newspapers print details about their lives, including things that are not true. When David has a bad game, soccer fans sometimes become angry with him. David handles the attention by focusing on soccer and his family.

David is often followed by fans and media who want to take his picture or get his autograph. It is difficult for David and his family to carry out their daily activities, such as shopping or eating at a restaurant.

David has Obsessive Compulsive **Disorder** (OCD). People with OCD have the same thoughts over and over again. This causes them great stress. They try to stop these thoughts by performing certain actions repeatedly. If they do not do this, they believe something bad will happen. People with OCD know their actions are unreasonable. Still, they continue. Some people with OCD wash their hands again and again. Others must count objects or actions. David needs objects to be arranged in straight lines or symmetrical patterns. He likes things to be in pairs. He will count the soda cans in his fridge again and again. If there is an uneven number, David will not be able to relax. Coping with his OCD takes up a great deal of David's time.

Many people with OCD try to hide their disorder from others. David shared his OCD with the world to let others know that they are not alone.

Like David, many people with OCD are successful in professional sports and the arts. They are good at repeatedly practicing skills. They are also able to focus on details.

Achievements and Successes

David's father loved the Manchester United team, so David grew up loving it, too. By the time David was four, he had told his friends and family that he was going to play soccer for Manchester United. David's greatest success is that his dream came true. He became one of the best athletes ever to play for Manchester United. He is one of the biggest soccer stars in the team's history.

David has won many awards. These include Young Player of the Year (1997), Britain's Sportsman of the Year (2001), and BBC Sports Personality of the Year (2001). David became a member of the Order of the British Empire in 2003. On June 25, 2006, David became the first English player to score in three World Cup tournaments. That same year, David was one of the best-paid athletes in the world. His contract with the L.A. Galaxy was worth $250 million over 5 years.

David has met many other influential people, including Nelson Mandela, the former president of South Africa. In 2003, David presented Mandela with a Team England soccer jersey.

David's success has allowed him to help others. In 2004, he and Victoria set up a **charity** that gives money to children in need around the world. The following year, David became a Goodwill **Ambassador** for the United Nations Children's Fund (UNICEF). In this role, David promotes sports and fitness to improve the lives of children in all parts of the world.

In 2005, David realized another lifelong goal when he opened the David Beckham Academy. This is a school for children who want to learn how to play soccer. David has said that, when he stops playing soccer professionally, he will spend most of his time teaching at his academy. David hopes to open soccer schools in many countries.

THE DAVID BECKHAM ACADEMY

The David Beckham Academy provides soccer camps for thousands of children in London, England, and Los Angeles, California. The camps are for children that are 8 to 15 years of age. Coaches train students in the rules and skills of soccer. They provide special training for those who want to learn a specific position, such as **midfielder** or goalie. Many of the academy's programs are free of charge. To learn more about the David Beckham Academy, visit **www.thedavidbeckhamacademy.com**.

Write a Biography

A person's life story can be the subject of a book. This kind of book is called a biography. Biographies describe the lives of remarkable people, such as those who have achieved great success or have done important things to help others. These people may be alive today or they may have lived many years ago. Reading a biography can help you learn more about a remarkable person.

At school, you might be asked to write a biography. First, decide who you want to write about. You can choose an athlete, such as David Beckham, or any other person you find interesting. Then, find out if your library has any books about this person. Learn as much as you can about him or her. Write down the key events in this person's life. What was this person's childhood like? What has he or she accomplished? What are his or her goals? What makes this person special or unusual?

A concept web is a useful research tool. Read the questions in the following concept web. Answer the questions in your notebook. Your answers will help you write your biography review.

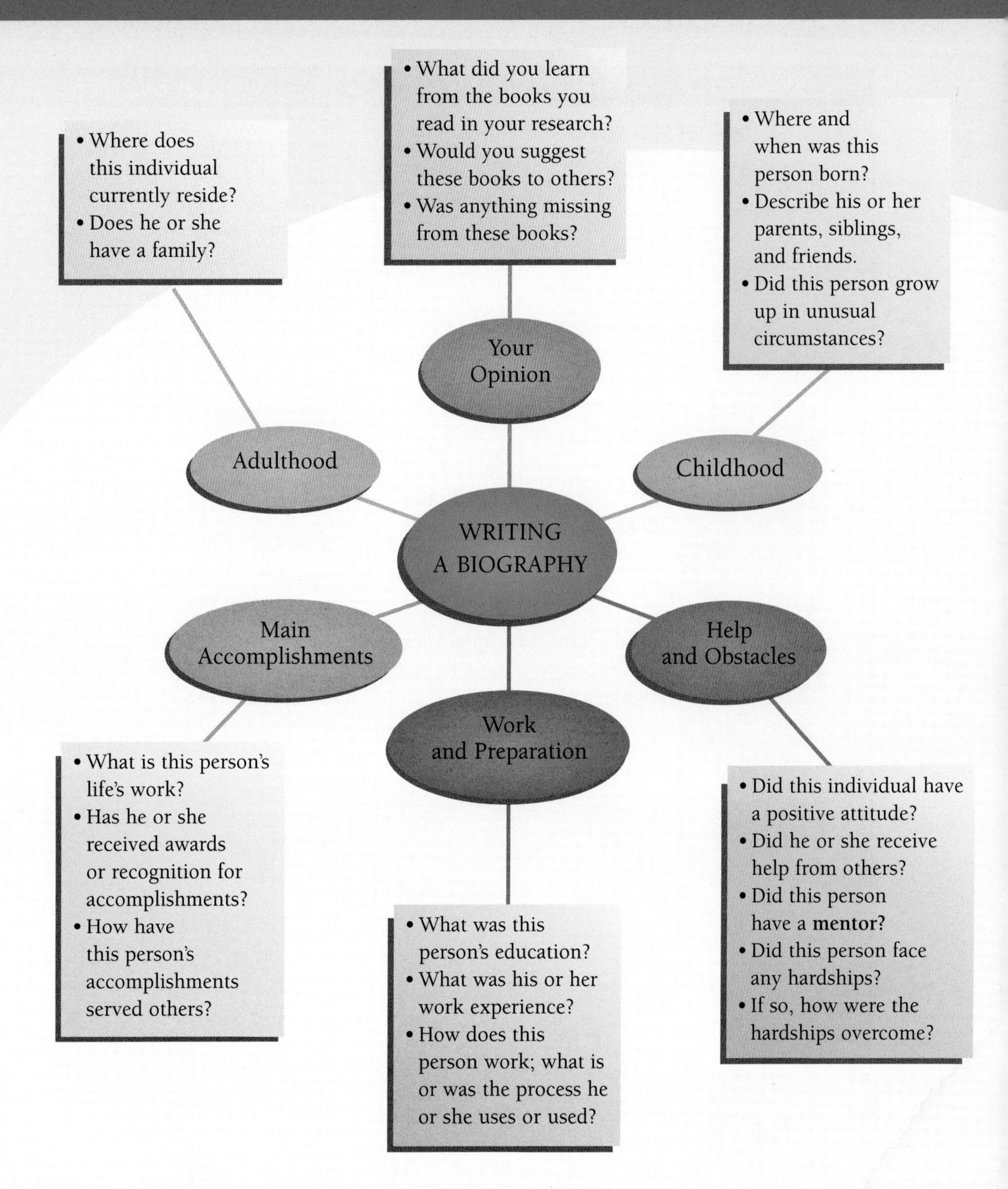
• What did you learn from the books you read in your research?
• Would you suggest these books to others?
• Was anything missing from these books?
• Where does this individual currently reside?
• Does he or she have a family?
• Where and when was this person born?
• Describe his or her parents, siblings, and friends.
• Did this person grow up in unusual circumstances?
Your Opinion
Adulthood
Childhood
WRITING A BIOGRAPHY
Main Accomplishments
Help and Obstacles
Work and Preparation
• What is this person's life's work?
• Has he or she received awards or recognition for accomplishments?
• How have this person's accomplishments served others?
• What was this person's education?
• What was his or her work experience?
• How does this person work; what is or was the process he or she uses or used?
• Did this individual have a positive attitude?
• Did he or she receive help from others?
• Did this person have a **mentor?**
• Did this person face any hardships?
• If so, how were the hardships overcome?

Timeline

YEAR	DAVID BECKHAM	WORLD EVENTS
1975	David is born on May 2.	On May 16, Junko Tabei of Japan becomes the first woman in the world to reach the top of Mount Everest.
1982	David joins the Ridgeway Rovers.	Scott Hamilton of the United States becomes the Men's World Figure Skating Champion for the second time in Copenhagen, Denmark.
1991	David signs with Manchester United on July 8.	The U.S. women's soccer team wins the first FIFA Women's World Cup tournament on November 30.
1996	David scores a key goal against Wimbledon on August 18. He becomes a star athlete.	Women's soccer is played at the Olympics for the first time, in Atlanta, Georgia.
1999	David marries Victoria Adams on July 4.	Mia Hamm scores her 108th goal on March 6.
2005	David opens the first David Beckham Academy on November 28.	On July 24, Lance Armstrong wins the Tour de France for the seventh time in a row.
2007	On January 11, David announces he will leave Real Madrid to join the Los Angeles Galaxy.	The Rugby World Cup takes place in France from September 7 to October 20. The event happens only once every four years.

Further Research

How can I find out more about David Beckham?

Most libraries have computers that connect to a database for searching for information. If you input a key word, you will be provided with a list of books in the library that contain information on that topic. Non-fiction books are arranged numerically, using their call number. Fiction books are organized alphabetically by the author's last name.

Websites

To learn more about David Beckham, visit http://la.galaxy.mlsnet.com

To learn more about soccer, visit www.ussoccer.com

Words to Know

ambassador: an official representative

charity: a fund for helping people in need
county: a local territory
crossbar: a horizontal beam that forms the top of the goal

disorder: an illness causing unusual functioning of the mind or body

FIFA: the Fédération Internationale de Football Association, which oversees the sport

goalie: the person who stands in the goal to prevent the opposing team from scoring

journalists: people who write news stories

matches: contests between teams
mentor: a wise and trusted teacher
midfielder: a player who moves the ball forward for others to kick into the goal; the position David Beckham plays

Premier League: the highest level of team soccer in the United Kingdom

professional: a person who earns money by doing an activity

scouts: people who are paid to find talented athletes to join professional sports teams
synthetic: made by people

tattooed: drawn with permanent dye on skin
teamwork: when members of a group act together to complete tasks
tournament: a contest or series of contests played for a championship

vision: the ability to look toward the future

Index